Shout for Joy!

Our Daily Bread
Publishing™

Requests for permission to quote from this book should be directed to: Permissions Department, Our Daily Bread Publishing, PO Box 3566, Grand Rapids, MI 49501, or contact us by email at permissionsdept@odb.org.

Library of Congress Cataloging-in-Publication Data available.

ISBN: 978-1-64070-121-2

Interior design by Patti Brinks

Printed in China

22 23 24 25 26 27 28 29 / 8 7 6 5 4 3 2 1

For Phoebe Yeh, who began my journey with me and ran
alongside me until my hand was safely planted in Joyce's.
And for Joyce M. Dinkins, who listened and heard what
He intended for me to bring to all children.
And for the children, both happy and suffering: God wants you
to SHOUT for JOY, for JOY will come in the morning!

Shout for joy to the Lord, everyone, everywhere.

Worship the Lord, and serve Him with joy.

Bring and sing to
God all your songs
of joy and praise.

Know in your mind and heart
that our Lord is a good God.

God is good
all the time.

God is our Maker, the Artist of us.
He is our Creator.
We belong to Him.

We are God's people.
We are His flock.

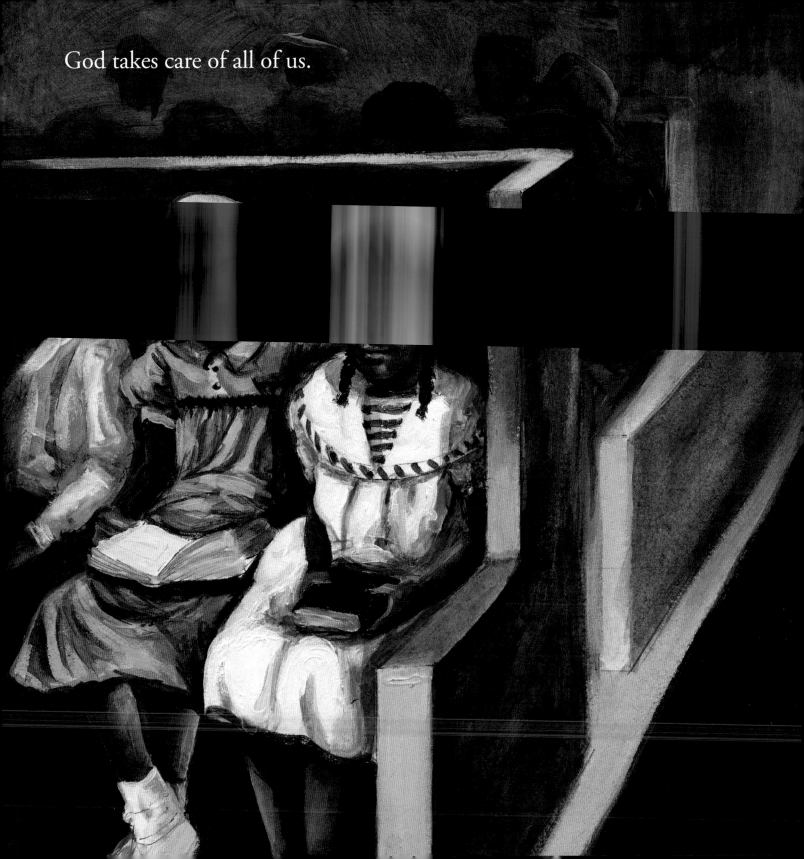

God takes care of all of us.

Come into His city with songs.

Come to God
with all our praises.

Honor God. Give God thanks.
Praise and worship Him day and night.
In the light and in the dark.

God, our Creator, is good!
He made everything that's good.

God's love is the best.
God's love for us is like
a never-ending rainbow.

We can trust God forever.
God watches over us.

God watches over every boy and girl.
Every one of us.
Every nation.
Every generation.

The Bible tells us so.

Paraphrase of Psalm 100

Shout for joy to the Lord, everyone, everywhere.

Worship the Lord, and serve Him with joy.

Bring and sing to God all your songs of joy and praise.

Know in your mind and heart that our Lord is a good God.

God is good all the time.

God is our Maker, the Artist of us.

He is our Creator. We belong to Him.

We are God's people. We are His flock.

God takes care of all of us.

Come into His city with songs.

Come to God with all our praises.

Honor God. Give God thanks.

Praise and worship Him day and night. In the light and in the dark.

God, our Creator, is good! He made everything that's good.

God's love is the best. God's love for us is like a never-ending rainbow.

We can trust God forever.

God watches over us.

God watches over every boy and girl.

Every one of us. Every nation. Every generation.

The Bible tells us so.